TESTED BY
TEMPTATION

TESTED BY TEMPTATION

by

W. Graham Scroggie

KREGEL PUBLICATIONS
Grand Rapids, Mi 49501

Tested by Temptation by W. Graham Scroggie.
Published by Kregel Publications,
a division of Kregel, Inc. All rights reserved.

Library of Congress Cataloging in Publication Data

Scroggie, William Graham, 1877-1958.
  Tested by Temptation.

  Reprint of the 1923 ed. published by Pickering and Inglis,
London.
    1. Jesus Christ—Temptation. 2. Temptation. I. Title.
BT355.S37 1980   232.9'5   79-2559
ISBN 0-8254-3732-6

Printed in the United States of America

CONTENTS

CONTENTS

1

TESTED BY TEMPTATION

THIS little volume has at least a threefold object. It is to feed our hungry souls; to fortify us against specious errors; and to fit us for Christian service. It is therefore designed to be not only inspirational, but instructive, and the subject of our studies may be called, 'Tested by Temptation.'

In Matt. iv. 1: we read, 'Then was Jesus led up by the Spirit into the wilderness to be tempted by the devil.' It has been truly said that the secret of Christianity lies in the personality of Jesus Christ. The more, therefore, that we know of Him, the better shall we understand it. In these studies we will consider our Lord's temptation in the wilderness, which, with true spiritual perception, Milton made the theme of his 'Paradise Regained.' From his doing this we are not to conclude that he conceived of our redemption as achieved in the wilderness rather than on the Cross; but that here he saw the beginning of the undoing of the damage wrought in Eden, and the promise and the power of its completion. We take up this meditation in simple reliance upon that same Holy Spirit by whom Jesus was led to His trial, and turning aside from vain speculations we shall keep the practical values of this event ever in view.

Before entering in detail upon the several temptations, a number of matters of great importance claim our attention, as, for instance, the record of this struggle; the combatants in it; the time, scene and duration of it; the necessity for it; and the appointment, design, and compass of it.

1. First of all, *the record of this struggle.* Two particulars here are of engaging interest and importance, namely, the mediate and immediate sources of our information. The mediate sources. The synoptic Gospels, with characteristic variation, all record the temptation; Mark's is the briefest. Matthew, who almost certainly follows the order of happening, places the temptation on the 'mountain' last, while Luke places it second. John does not mention the event at all, a fact to be accounted for by the whole view and purpose of his Gospel. But, seeing that neither of the Evangelists, nor any others were present to witness this great struggle, from whence did they get their information? Here we are thrown back upon the immediate source, which must have been Christ Himself. If the temptation be authentic, the account must have come originally from the lips of the Lord Himself. Here, therefore, we have a wonderful and mysterious revelation of a profound experience in Christ's spiritual life, and it becomes us to approach the study of it with reverent expectation. What He has been pleased to tell us we must believe, and what He has been pleased to conceal we should not make the subject of speculation, or the ground of unbelief.

2. The next thing that claims our attention is *the combatants in this struggle.* Note the first and last words of the verse: '*Jesus* was led up by the Spirit into the wilderness to be tempted by the *devil.*' *Jesus*, the

name in this connection is of great importance. It
was not as the Divine Son of God clothed with glory
that He entered into the wilderness, although the
Father had recently borne witness to His Sonship;
neither was it as the Christ anointed for service,
although He had just received that anointing with the
Holy Spirit; neither was it as the Lord, 'Who, by
inheritance has obtained a better name and place
than the angels,' and before Whom all yet must bow
and own His Lordship, though that name is guaranteed
to Him by the Father. But it was Jesus, the name that
tells us of His humanity, that brings Him into sympa-
thetic touch with us and announces His purpose to
save. From this we see that Jesus was led into the
conflict as man, and not as God. In the fourth
Gospel, which opens with a sublime declaration of
Christ's Deity, there is no reference to the temptation,
as we have said. Satan twice appealed to Him as the
Divine Son in the words, 'If Thou be the Son of God';
but Jesus absolutely refused to be drawn on to that
ground, not out of consideration for the devil, but for
us. The whole value to us of the temptation consists
in this fact; for had Christ fought out that battle on
ground we could never occupy, and in a strength we
do not possess, it could never have been said of Him,
'He was tempted in all points, like as we are, yet
without sin'; neither, again, 'In that He Himself
hath suffered, being tempted, He is able to succour
them that are tempted.' That great battle was
fought out and won by Jesus, not only as a necessary
self-discipline and preparation for the mission upon
which He was about to enter, but also as our representative and champion. This could not have been

had He met the enemy on any ground other than that of His humanity. Had He met the devil as the Divine Son He would have proved to be his Lord, but not our Deliverer.

This leads to another important truth, namely, because Jesus was Man the ordeal was terribly real to Him. Perhaps it is inevitable to wonder how the sinless Christ could be in any real sense the subject of temptation. A hot controversy was waged around this question in the Middle Ages, some taking the view that Christ could not have sinned, and others that He could. The one thing that emerges clearly is that He had the power not to sin, and that was the power which humanity most urgently needed. We have no means of knowing what form the temptation took further than is indicated by the words which record it. But that it was an awful assault upon Christ's sinless and sensitive human nature, utterly repugnant and exquisitely painful, is beyond all question; and that is all we need to know on the point. The fact that the record is autobiographical is conclusive both for its authenticity and the painful reality of what occurred.

Now, let us turn our attention to Jesus' enemy, the *devil*. The narrative should be conclusive as to the fact of his personality. If the Bible be true, Satan is an evil person and not merely an evil influence. There is as much evidence for believing in the personality of the devil as in the personality of God. This is witnessed to by the titles applied to him, by the works attributed to him, and by the judgment pronounced against him. Never in Scripture is the word 'devil' used to personify evil in either man or the world, but always to signify an evil, personal spirit. Those who offer him little or no resistance are inclined to deny his existence.

The devil's last trick was to spread the report of his own death. He is not what Giovanni Papini refers to as a ridiculous invention of the Church to induce repentance; he is a personal and fierce antagonist of all who will not follow him. Goethe's Mephistopheles wants to know what is the profit of getting rid of the devil so long as the devilish remains. What is the use of explaining away the Evil One so long as the evil ones who remain are so many? No; it was a personal devil that met the personal Saviour in the wilderness, and the role which he there assumed was that of Diabolus, the caluminator, the traducer, the overthrower.

What may we say of the range of his knowledge? We dare not underestimate the knowledge of him whom the Scriptures reveal, and whom the history of man proves to be a being of vast intelligence; and nowhere is that intelligence more evident than in the temptation of our Lord. But, on the other hand, we must not over-estimate his knowledge, for whereas he has much understanding of the Divine purposes he is obviously ignorant of the Divine resources. This is one of the comforting truths which this narrative furnishes. And there is another which bears upon the extent of his power. This, it must be admitted, is vast. He is the prince of the demons, the god of this age, the prince of the power of the air, the ruler of the darkness of this world. These are fearsome glimpses of the extent of his power. Yet, vast though it be, it is Divinely restricted. God says to him, as to the uprushing tide, 'So far shalt thou come, and no farther.' We shall not forget the case of Job in evidence of this. But the greatest and most comforting evidence of the limitations of the devil's power is found in the narrative before us. Christ at His lowest vanquished the devil at his highest; the Saviour at His weakest routed His adversity at his strongest, thereby proving the limitation of the enemy's power and the extent of our own in Christ. *Jesus* and the *devil*. What a conjunction! The Father and the World, the Spirit and the Flesh, Jesus and the Devil, are set over against one another, and the antitheses are most impressive. The most important and awful battles that have ever been fought are the two between Jesus and Diabolus, the one in the wilderness, and the other in the garden. There the Prince of Light and the prince of darkness met in deadly combat to decide the issue as between truth and error, right and wrong, heaven and hell, and, as there Jesus represented us, our fate depended upon the issue. These, then, are the antagonists who fought out, unseen by mortal eye, in dread and deadly fashion, the battle of the ages wherein the last Adam won back for us the paradise which the first Adam lost, and opened up the way for our deliverance.

3. Let us now observe *the time of this struggle*. Our chapter opens impressively with the word 'then,' and, naturally, we ask, When? To this inquiry there is a double answer. It was after and before. It was after the baptism. This was an act of obedience to the will of God in pursuit of the fulfilment of 'all righteousness,' and therefore was not likely to go unchallenged by the enemy. He who most closely

follows God will be most closely followed by the devil. Never can we engage in any act of true surrender without exposing ourselves to the onslaught of this great foe. You have but to pursue the path of loyal obedience to the known will of God and you shall certainly have Diabolus in hot pursuit of you. Also, it was after the bestowal. This was an endowment of power for service, and, therefore, a definite challenge to the prince of darkness, for Christ came to destroy the works of the devil. It is only to be expected that anointing shall be followed by assault, that after the Dove shall come the devil. John Bunyan wisely places the Valley of Humiliation and the wrestling with Apollyon, after the sweet refreshment of the Beautiful House, with all its holy communings. The old highway robbers never took any risk with a poor man, but always watched for one who had plenty of money upon him. In like manner it is the new convert, the rich soul, the successful Christian worker, that the devil attacks, for he would rob us of our riches.

Further, it was after the benediction. This was an expression of God's pleasure in Jesus, and an attestation of His Divine Sonship. But after the benediction comes the battle. The devil always most opposes those whom God most approves.

It is those who are obedient, endowed, and well-pleasing to God who are the especial objects of the enemy's stratagems. To be left unmolested by Satan is no evidence of spiritual vigour. Seasons of fiercest temptation frequently follow seasons of greatest blessing. Worship is often the path to war.

But fully to apprehend the significance of this struggle we must see it not only as coming after, but also *before* momentous events. Perhaps it was what lay before Christ that troubled the devil more than what lay behind. Our Lord was just about to enter upon His public-service life, and this fact, with all that it signified, would be well known to the devil. If by any means he could disqualify One so capable of doing his kingdom such harm he would do so. They who are negligent of, or indolent in, the service of Christ are not likely to be troubled by the devil. He directs his diabolical genius against those only who are formidable, who are in any sense able to engage such a champion; yet at no time did his intention so miscarry as on this occasion. The means designed to disqualify but qualified the Christ. This conflict with its issues furnished the ground for the service-life of Jesus. He was on the threshold of His ministry, facing His life-work with all its infinite issues, and there was a needs-be that His quality be tried. It must be seen whether He was fit for so great a task. By means, therefore, of what the devil meant for injury was Jesus tested and found true. Winning, He was shown to be worthy; conquering, He was competent to lead. In like manner everyone who would be used must be tried. As the bridge is proved by the weight, and the gold by the fire, so man is proved by temptation. Martin Luther would never have been the man he was but for the devil. We therefore should not be surprised if, early and late in our Christian life, we are put to ever fresh tests; rather should we regard this as a providential means whereby we are qualified for wider and better service. Between our worship and our work we must be ready for war.

This conflict revealed the secret of the service-life

of Jesus. He did at the beginning what He purposed to do throughout; He started as He would continue. Right at the heart of His achievement and endurance were unbending loyalty to the truth as revealed, and absolute devotion to His Father. By these canons we should test alike our life and our service, finding in their presence the secret of our success, and in their absence the explanation of our failure. I said, 'we should test'; but there will be no need, for the devil will do it for us. It is the temptation to disloyalty that will draw loyalty into the open, and the inducement to treachery that will call devotion into action.

Necessary and enriching therefore are the assaults of the devil. And so we see that this conflict struck the key-note of the service-life of Jesus. Had He failed here He would have failed everywhere; but there was no defeat in His life—every conflict issued in conquest; every battle brought blessing, and every temptation was turned to triumph. This would be more often so with ourselves were we more alive to the devices of the devil. The tempter is a master in his choice of hours, and, although he may come at any time, there are certain times when almost certainly he will come. In and after seasons of special blessing we should be specially watchful, and on the eve of every holy enterprise. Attack follows attestation, and conflict precedes service.

4. And now observe *the scene of this struggle*. This is of deeper significance than might at first appear. 'Jesus was led up into the *wilderness* to be tempted by the devil.' Where exactly it was to which Jesus retired for this solemn experience matters little, though

we have no reason for rejecting the traditional place 'in the wilderness that goeth up from Jericho.' The thing of importance is that it was a 'wilderness,' and this, not of co-incidence or accident, but, we must believe, of infinitely wise design. We should remember that the wilderness is a producer of man's sin. God said to Adam, 'Cursed is the ground for thy sake.'

All barrenness and abortion are the hallmarks of sin in the outward creation, and it would seem that these desolated places are the especial haunts of evil spirits. It was not in a wilderness that the first Adam was tempted, but in a garden, and there, being overcome, we, with all the race, became inhabitants of a cursed earth, of which the wilderness is the final expression. On the other hand, it was not in a garden that the last Adam was tempted, but in a wilderness, and there, taking up the conflict exactly where the first Adam had left it, and inheriting all the consequences of his defeat, Jesus conquered the devil and won back the garden for that race whose champion and representattive in the conflict He had been. These unquestionable facts for ever brand as false the teaching that all man needs for the development of the goodness within him is a suitable environment. History does not confirm that theory. Paradise was lost in a garden and regained in a wilderness. In spite of every circumstance being favourable to good in Eden, Adam and Eve failed; and in spite of every circumstance motioning to evil in the wilderness, Christ stood, and so proclaimed for ever that there is a power by which we may triumph over every disability and conquer every foe. But again, the wilderness is a reflection of our fallen nature. It is, as one

has said, the echo in the outward world of the desola-
tion and *wasteness* which sin has wrought in the inner
life of man. It reflects our fallen nature in its wasteness, for the soul, as the wilderness, left to nature
uncultivated, is productive of all manner of rank and
wild growths. It represents also our sinful nature in
its *terrors,* for, as in the wilderness may be heard the
cries of wild birds and beasts, so in the soul may be
heard the terrifying voices of conscience and reason,
which proclaim the certainty of judgment, and speak
of death to the unrepentant.

But mercifully the wilderness represents also our
sinful self in its *possibilities*. It is much more true of
the inward than of the outward realm that 'instead
of the thorn may come up the fir tree, and instead of
the brier may come up the myrtle tree'; 'that the
barren ground may become a pool, and the thirsty
land springs of water; that in the habitation of
dragons may be grass with reeds and rushes';
and 'that the wilderness may blossom as the rose.'
All this has been made gloriously possible by Him to
Whom the wilderness was a sanctuary, and in Whose
presence the very beasts were tame. Plainly it was of
purpose that this struggle was entered upon in the
wilderness—a place that speaks so loudly, literally
and figuratively, of man's defeat.

But, still further, the wilderness is suggestive of all
human conflict. In all ages there have been men who
have sought in retirement immunity from the temptations of public life, and who have thought to escape
evil by changing their place. But is it not true that our
fiercest struggles are experienced in solitude? Away
from the crowd and bustle of life we may be free from

the snares of wealth and fashion and pleasure; but it is only to be met by other snares more insidious and concealed. If the city lays our soul open to assault on one side, certainly the wilderness exposes us on another. If Christ, without that within Him on which temptation might play, was thus fiercely assailed, where can we hope to go from temptation who carry within us the conditions which give it every promise of success? David, who had engaged many a foe, and nobly won many a battle against both man and beast, succumbed to the beast within him in an hour of solitude. We should ever remember that it is in private that we are prepared for our defeats or victories in public. But while bearing in mind the peculiar perils of solitude we cannot over-estimate its educative value. Foundations are always out of sight, and it is ever in seclusion from the crowd that the foundations of character and service, good or evil, are laid. In evidence we have only to think of Jacob by the Jabbok, of Moses and Elijah at Horeb, and of Jesus in the wilderness. How eminently fitting it was that our great Leader should have fought and won in that solitude where all our greatest battles must be fought, for ever to teach us that there is no place where we may not always conquer every evil.

5. Nor must we pass as insignificant *the duration of this struggle*. 'Forty days and forty nights.' The frequency of the number 'forty' in Scripture, and in certain connections, compels us to the conclusion that it has a moral significance. There were three periods of forty years in the life of Moses; the first three kings of Israel each reigned for forty

years; the Israelites were in the wilderness for
forty years; from the Crucifixion to the Destruction
of Jerusalem was a period of forty years; Moses
was twice in the Mount for forty days; Elijah
was for forty days at Horeb; and Jonah's message to
Nineveh proclaimed judgment in forty days. Also,
there were three periods of forty days each in the life
of our Lord; before His presentation in the Temple;
before the commencement of His public ministry;
and before His ascension into Heaven. A careful
comparison of these and other passages will show that
this period, whether of days or of years, is usually one
of probation, or preparation, or punishment. Certainly in the case of our blessed Lord, it was a period
of final preparation ere He entered upon that brief
ministry which was to issue in the Cross. It was a
period at once of temptation and equipment; of
discipline and demonstration.

Unless careful attention is paid to the united text
of the Evangelists, we are likely to fall into one of two
errors: by supposing either, that the temptations here
recorded covered a period of forty days; or, that Jesus
was tempted only on the fortieth day. Both these
conceptions are contrary to the facts, which are, that
the temptations of the record were all on the fortieth
day, but that Jesus was tempted during all the pre-
ceding thirty-nine days. 'He was in the wilderness
forty days, tempted of Satan.' In these facts is a
wealth of comfort for tempted men and women like
ourselves. Such a crisis as our Lord's fortieth day
comes sooner or later to each of us, and, although
terribly severe while it lasts, it is often bravely and
successfully faced. We are enabled to rise to the great

occasion. But if Jesus had endured only this short and sharp conflict we would be justified in feeling that His experience hardly represented our own, and that His victory was scarcely typical, for it is not *the fortieth day* that we fear so much as *the thirty-nine days* of petty assault, of guerilla warfare, of irritating trial. A great field-day appeals to our imagination, and inspires us to supreme effort, but it is to the countless, nameless, petty battles of the thirty-nine days that we usually succumb. But Jesus faced these also. In ways of which we have no record, He was assailed by the devil during the whole period, and the fortieth-day temptations were but the last, concentrated, and desperate assault of the infuriated foe upon His weakened body but loyal spirit.

We can understand only very partially how depressing an influence upon Jesus was the presence of the devil. Margaret, in Faust, felt this withering influence of Mephistopheles:—

> His presence chills my blood;
> Besides, when he is near I ne'er could pray,
> And this it is that eats my heart away.

We are not wholly unacquainted with this experience. There are some people who, by their presence, freeze our buoyancy; there are some deadly influences that damp our ardour. Missionaries have said that, in places where they were serving, the air seemed to be electric with evil spirits, and that they seemed to be placed 'where Satan's seat is.' That is the experience of the thirty-nine days, and Jesus knew all about it. There is at least as much comfort in the unwritten part of this story as in what is recorded, for we see our Lord representing us, and showing us how to conquer, not only on the great and *special days* but throughout the countless *average days* of our Christian life.

6. But it is natural to enquire into *the necessity for this struggle*. We shall find necessity for it in Christ's sacred humanity. Because He was truly Man, He was subjected, as all men must be, to moral discipline. The essential characteristic of all that is best in human nature is growth; this is the law of life alike for body and soul. Our moral and spiritual powers are not developed except by exercise and experience; and it was not otherwise with our Master.

> Though He were a Son, yet learned He obedience by the things which He suffered.

That Jesus grew physically does not imply that His body was either diseased or deformed; and that He grew morally does not imply in Him any taint of sin or moral imperfection. There was a profound necessity, and we must frankly recognise it, that our Lord's pure and stainless humanity 'be disciplined by sorrow, matured by conflict, strengthened by endurance, and perfected by patience.' This discipline extended over the whole period of His life. It was in progress during the thirty years at Nazareth, when the foundations were laid in knowledge on which His ministry was to be built. It certainly was in progress during the years of that sublime ministry, for He speaks of His disciples' fellowship with Him in His temptations, and these do not include either the wilderness or the garden experiences. But there were both reason and necessity for the desperate ordeal through which He passed ere He emerged from private into public life; a necessity that was personal and moral.

But beyond this, we shall find necessity for it in His saving mission. He who would help us must understand us. His experience, in all essentials, must lie alongside our own. And so we read that, 'He, having suffered, being tempted, is able to succour them that are tempted.' And again, 'We have not a High Priest Who cannot be touched with the feeling of our infirmities, but Who was in all points tempted like as we are, sin apart.' We cannot afford to forget that this battle was fought out by our Lord on the field of our humanity, and won by forces available to every child of man. Christ was led into the wilderness, not only for His personal discipline, but also for our deliverance. The antagonist of the devil was the representative of men, and there, in mortal conflict, He dealt a deadly blow at the enemy's power, and lit the fires of hope in all our hearts. And yet again, there was a necessity for it in His eternal purpose. The two foregoing, the discipline of His sacred humanity, and His struggle as the representative of men, were in pursuance of His eternal purpose, but the purpose itself was larger than them both. It involved issues that lie beyond our present knowledge, and of which we have only scattered intimations. The presence of evil in the universe is an age-long and unsolved mystery, and what God ultimately will do with it we do not know; but one thing, at least, stands clear of all doubt, namely, that by means of the experience of Bethlehem, and the Wilderness, and Calvary, and the Resurrection, the works of the devil are doomed to destruction, and the devil himself to utter and eternal defeat. The struggle and victory of Christ in the wilderness brought nearer, and made more sure, that

day when all things shall be 'headed up' in Him,
things in the heavens, in the earth, and under the
earth, and when all tongues shall confess that He is
Lord to the glory of God the Father.

7. But we have by no means exhausted the preliminary considerations. We must not overlook *the
appointment of this struggle.* 'Then was Jesus led up by
the Spirit into the wilderness.' It is well to recall
the general fact that the Holy Spirit filled and con-
trolled the life of Jesus. By that Spirit He was be-
gotten, and was endued for service; by the Spirit He
preached the Gospel and wrought miracles; and by
the Spirit He offered Himself in death, and was raised
from the dead. His was a life Spirit-filled, and a
service Spirit-directed. The Holy Spirit was not
given to Him by measure, and there never was a time
when His possession of the Spirit was less than His
capacity. This general fact prepares us for the particular fact that the Spirit led Jesus to be tempted. We
assume that it is not His own personal spirit that is
here referred to, but the Holy Spirit, the third blessed
Person of the Trinity. FATHER, SON, and SPIRIT are
here revealed as co-operating for our redemption;
the FATHER bearing witness to His Son; the SON
receiving the enduement of the Spirit; and the SPIRIT
leading the Son to His great trial. Jesus is led by the
DOVE to conflict with the DEVIL. He was led by the
Good Spirit to be tempted by the Evil Spirit. The
words employed to set this forth are noteworthy.
Luke says that He was 'led'; Matthew says that He
was 'led up'; Mark says that He was 'driven.' Jesus
being 'led' points to the fact that He was directed; His

being 'driven,' to the manner in which He was directed.
That He was 'led' signifies the concurrence of His will
with the motions of the Spirit; that He was 'driven'
signifies that He was taken thither suddenly and by a
vehement impulse, and that He shrank from it.   It
is worthy of note that Jesus did not 'go' into temptation, He 'fell' into it.   He did not run to meet the
devil, but was directed by the Divine Spirit to where
the devil would meet Him.   Our blessèd Lord was at
the disposal of the Holy Spirit.   'As the wind blows
in the unfolded canvas of a ship and bears her power-
fully along, so the Divine afflatus blew quite a gale in
the outstretched faculties of the Saviour, and carried
Him out of public view into the solitude of the wilderness' for the purpose of temptation.   His own and the
Spirit's will were not in conflict; for if the 'leading'
was 'driving' assuredly the 'driving' was 'leading.'

The practical teaching arising out of this fact is of
ever-pressing importance to us all.   It teaches us
what our relation should be to temptation.   Let it be
said, first of all, that temptation is never to be sought.
It was after His terrible experience that our Lord
taught His disciples to pray 'lead us not into temptation'; and then, as if remembering that He Himself
was led into it, and that we might be, He added, 'but
deliver us from the Evil One.'   There is no need for
us to seek temptation; it will soon enough, and successfully enough, seek us.   But beyond this, let it be
said that, temptation is ever to be shunned.   Speaking
of evil assaults, Paul, writing to Timothy, says, 'But
thou, O man of God, flee these things.'   It sometimes
takes more courage to 'flee' than to 'fight'; and, in
any case, it is no use fighting when we should flee,

for then we have no promise of protection or deliverance. Temptation is a serious matter, and the soul that knows its susceptibility to it will never court it, but cut it; will never seek it, but shun it. Yet, though we do not seek it, and while we shun it, it will come; and so, still further, let it be said that temptation is always to be endured. 'Blessed is the man that endureth temptation; for when he is tried he shall receive the crown of life which the Lord has promised to them that love Him' (James i. 12). In that glorious eleventh chapter of the Hebrews, the heroes of faith are of two classes—those who, by faith, achieved; and those who, by faith, endured; and the most eloquent passage in the chapter is that which tells of those who endured. 'They were stoned, they were sawn asunder, were tempted, were slain with the sword . . . of whom the world was not worthy.' To endure is to suffer without yielding, to hold out, and at last to emerge victoriously. This our Lord did, and this He bids us do, and enables us to do; for, 'There hath no temptation taken you but such as is common to man; but God is faithful, Who will not suffer you to be tempted above that ye are able; but will with the temptation also make a way to escape, that ye may be able to bear it' (1 Cor. x. 13). To deliberately go into temptation, or, being led of the Spirit into it, to yield to it, is the way of certain defeat. Our only infallible safeguard is entire subjection to the Spirit of God, Who will direct us as to conflict, equip us for it, and keep us trustful in it. The presence of temptation, the sore pressure of the Evil One, is no evidence of a disposition to sin on our part, but may be, and often is, a Divine appointment for our more rapid perfecting.

8. That leads us to think of *the design of this struggle.* This is different as we view the occasion from the standpoint of God or of the devil. The words 'to tempt,' and 'temptation,' are not used in the New Testament with a uniform significance, but sometimes mean, 'to try, or prove,' and sometimes, 'to allure, or seduce.' There is another word which has the former only of these two meanings, and is reserved for the idea of being tested to be found worthy. But the word used in our text sometimes refers to the privations, sorrows, and sufferings, or the storms of persecution, which the Christian must endure, and which are designed to prove his moral courage and worth; and sometimes it refers to the enticements to sin, in whatever form and from whatever quarter, which have for their end our overthrow. Temptation in the one view alarms us, and in the other it allures us. In the one instance the proving is in order to disprove, and in the other it is in order to approve. This distinction of meanings is of the greatest importance, and must be apprehended if we would fully understand the significance of our Lord's Temptation. However difficult it may be to understand it, the fact remains that *Jesus was tempted.* Concerning this, the narrative leaves us in no doubt . 'He was led up by the Spirit into the wilderness *to be tempted by the devil.*' The devil approached Jesus with malicious hope of moving Him from His loyal obedience to the will of God; of causing Him to doubt His Father's love, and desert His cause. He who would bear the burden of sin's guilt must feel the force of sin's temptation. Christ could not be thoroughly tried without being tempted; but let us remember that the trial and the temptation, though

found in one and the same occasion, are different, alike in their origin and design. Jesus was tried throughout the whole of His life on earth, but He was not tempted all the time. The devil 'left Him for a season,' renewing the attack on the eve of the Transfiguration (Mark viii. 33), in Gethsemane, and at Calvary. So far as we know, these are the only occasions when the fiery darts of evil suggestion invaded the Saviour's soul, to be instantly quenched and repelled by the shield of faith and of prayer.

It is temptation as enticement to sin that is dominant in this story; and we need no other explanation of the fact than that which our own experience furnishes, when we remember that Jesus was there as our representative. But we cannot afford to overlook the fact that by this same occasion Jesus was tested. If it be true that He was 'led up by the Spirit to be tempted by the devil,' it is also true that He was assailed by the devil to be tried by the Spirit. About to enter upon His life's work, it was necessary that His capacity for it and worthiness of it should be proved. The lines of diabolical temptation were also the lines of Divine testing. The occasion whereby the devil would have Christ disproved was that whereby God found Him approved. Every test is not a temptation; but every temptation is a test. Trial of any sort must have one of two issues; either we stand, or we fall. Everything of moral worth is tested: the soldier by the battle; the runner by the track; the student by the examination; the heart by the truth. The refiner does not throw his ore into the pot except for the purpose that, whatever of dross may be found mingled with it may be drawn off and the precious metal come forth pure from the fiery trial. In the case of all of us, testing is in order to make us pure; but in the case of Jesus Christ, it was in order to prove Him pure. The Temptation in the wilderness was a revelation of character, and a disclosure of power; it brought to the light what Jesus really was, and could do. At the commencement of the ordeal, our Lord had the plenitude of the Spirit, but at the end He had the power of the Spirit. We read: 'He returned unto Galilee in the power of the Spirit.' As it was with Christ, so it is with us; equipment means exposure, and exposure faced and fought, as by our Lord, will lead to that true expansion of life and service which is none other than God's plan for us.

9. Before considering the several assaults of the one great Temptation, one other matter claims our attention, namely, *the compass of this struggle.* In view of the personal significance of this encounter, we might reasonably assume that, in some sense, the temptations of our Lord were comprehensive and exhaustive; and this, surely, is what is declared in the words, 'He was in all things tempted according to our likeness' (Heb. iv. 15). This cannot possibly mean that He was tempted in all the ways in which we are. We know He was not, for He did not sustain all the relations which we do, and every relation brings its own temptations. But it surely does mean that temptation assailed Him on all levels, so to speak, of His complex nature. There is no class or type of temptation known to us, which He was not made to feel. Temptation swept the whole field of His consciousness: His body, or sense-consciousness; His soul, or self-consciousness; His spirit, or God-consciousness. And as there is in

none of us any other consciousness, we see that temptation spent itself upon Him, our great representative. The duration of the Temptation was its length; the intensity of it was its depth; and the range, or compass of it, was its breadth. Christ 'suffered, being tempted,' and all the more because of 'the Divine volume of being within Him.' In His brief life He sustained the whole force of every temptation which may possibly assail humanity.

It has been impressively said that 'He lived through life.' The majority of men live only through a small portion of life. A man spends eighty years in the world, and yet, at the end of that long term, vast tracts of experience remain which he has not touched. But Christ traversed every region of life. In some thirty-five years He exhausted every emotion it is possible for man to experience. Had He lived a hundred years longer, there would have been no new regions of experience for Him to explore. He finished living ere He began dying, and then He finished dying, and emerged triumphantly on the other side. He traversed the whole continent of finite existence, yet 'without sin.' It was not until the devil 'had ended every kind of temptation,' according to St. Luke, that he departed. And so we turn to this record to learn how terribly real a fact is sin; how terrific is the force of temptation; how subtle and powerful is the arch-enemy of our souls; how glorious or tragic are the possibilities of solitude; how imminent is danger in the hour of exaltation; how closely intertwined are temptation and testing; how complete and final was the victory of Christ; and how sure is our triumph by faith in the means.

2

TEMPTATION TO SELFISHNESS

WE shall turn now to the first of the three temptations of our Lord, and read the texts, according
to Matthew's and Luke's records. In Matt. iv. 3, 4:
'The tempter, having come to Jesus, said, If Thou art
the Son of God, speak that these stones may become
loaves. But He answering said, It has been written,
Not by bread alone shall man live, but by every word
that proceedeth out of the mouth of God.'

In Luke iv. 3, 4: 'The devil said to Him, If Thou
art the Son of God, speak to this stone that it become
bread. Jesus answered unto him, saying, It has been
written that not on bread alone shall man live, but on
every word of God.'

There are one or two preliminary matters which
we must consider before turning to this first of the
three temptations. First of all, with reference to the
necessity and unity of the temptations. Perhaps no
feature of Christ's life has been a subject of greater
study than His temptation. That He could have been
tempted, as here revealed, has been a baffling mystery
to many devout minds. But it must be recognised
that temptation is a cardinal element in human
experience, and so that our Lord, by His incarnation,
subjected Himself to this experience and to every
other known to man, alike subjective and objective,
yet apart from sin. It is only by His having shared
our experiences that He is able to succour us. His

exposure to temptation was immediately and primarily constitutional, and not vocational. The temptations of our Lord were real and natural, and not professional or artificial. Because He was like us, His temptations were like ours, and are to be taken as the norm of ours.

But the question naturally arises, Were these temptations unrelated assaults of the Evil One? Or were they one assault representing three aspects of the same principle? In other words, are they to be likened to three beads on a string, or to three branches on a tree springing out of the same trunk and having the same root? Undoubtedly the latter is the true conception, and the unity of the temptations is found in the concentrated efforts of the devil to break down Christ's life of trust in God His Father—to break down, in the first temptation, the simplicity of that trust; in the second temptation, the sanity of that trust; and in the third temptation, the stability of that trust; in all which efforts the enemy ignominiously failed.

Certain things should be observed with reference to the assaults upon Jesus which have their correspondence in our own temptations. The attack was not made along the avenues of any gross or sinful desires, but was directed upon certain elementary needs or impulses of our nature which were essential factors of our Lord's humanity. Further, the attack was veiled under the guise of religion and of principle. The devil said, 'If Thou be the Son of God.' There, was a subtle blend of truth and error. Some truth there was, but mashed and brewed with lies. Yet further, the attack arose in the course of Jesus' devout meditation on His future work, and was directed against it, as well as against Him.

In like manner we are approached and attacked. Not always are we tempted directly to sin. Often are we tempted under the guise of religion and on the ground of principle, and frequently in hours of exaltation and of ecstasy, in times of fellowship and communion with God. There is a striking connection between the Eden temptation and this, alike in the way of comparison and contrast. In both cases the attack was made by Satan; in both the parties were representative; in both the appeal was made to the physical appetite; and in both the attack was made ostensibly in the interests of the parties attacked. This connection is significant and impressive. For, as Augustine has said, the entire history of the moral and spiritual world revolves around two persons—Adam and Christ.

As we further meditate on this passage we shall be impressed with the fact that He Who was the Bread of Life began His ministry by hungering, and He Who was the Water of Life ended His ministry by thirsting. Gregory of Nazianzus has beautifully developed this idea in these words: 'Christ hungered as man, and fed the hungry as God. He was hungry as man, and yet He is the Bread of Life; He was athirst as man, and yet He says, 'Let him that is athirst come unto Me and drink'; He was weary, and yet He is our rest; He pays tribute, and yet He is a King; He is called a devil, and casts out devils; He prays, and yet hears prayer; He weeps, and dries our tears; He is sold for thirty pieces of silver, and redeems the world; He is 'led as a sheep to the slaughter,' and is the Good Shepherd; He is mute like a sheep, and yet He is the Everlasting Word;

He is the 'man of sorrows,' but He heals our pains;
He is nailed to a Tree and dies upon it, and by the Tree
restores us to life; He has vinegar to drink, and changes
the water into wine; He lays down His life, and takes
it again; He dies, and gives life, and by dying destroys
death.'

Surveying the Temptation as whole, we see how
thoroughly comprehensive and universal it is. It
makes appeal to all the elements of our personality—
the first to our body; the second to our soul; the third
to our spirit. It appeals also to our three great
faculties—the first to our faith; the second to our
reason; the third to our conscience. It works upon
typical perils to which we are all exposed—the peril, in
the first, of appetite; in the second, of adventure; in the
third, of ambition. It uses all the constituent elements
of the world which threaten us—in the first, the lust
of the flesh; in the second, the lust of the eyes; in the
third, the pride of life. It seeks to degrade certain
legitimate desires—in the first, the desire for satis-
faction; in the second, the desire for acknowledgment;
in the third, the desire for usefulness. The Temptation
bears upon and seeks to damage our true relation—
in the first to God; in the second to the Church and
His people; in the third to the world.

1. Let us consider quite broadly the significance of
the first Temptation, and then the secret of Christ's
triumph. 'If Thou be the Son of God, command
that these stones be made bread.' Here we have a
threefold significance—primary, immediate, and ultimate. (i) The *primary significance* involves the principle
of obediemce to the will of God. The natural back-

ground of this temptation is the history of Israel as
recorded in Deut. vi.—xi., and especially to chapter
eight, verses two and three, which reveal the fact that
they, like Jesus, were tested by hunger, and that the
purpose was to know what was in their heart, whether
they would keep God's commandments or no.   God's
dealings with Israel were designed to test their conception of their relation to Him and His relation to
them, and all that was involved in that relation.   That
design lies aback also of this test of Jesus, and of every
man's, for we are all constituted by and for the will
and glory of God.   Frequently the immediate occasion
of the test is relatively small.   In the case of Adam and
Eve, of the Israelites in the wilderness, and of Jesus in
the wilderness, it was *food*.   But the profoundest
principle is involved nevertheless.   This experience
of Jesus is not primarily a tempting of Him by the
devil, so much as a testing of Him by the Father, and,
as in the case of Israel, it was both evidential and educative.   It was designed to test His conception of the
filial relation and to prove His possession of the filial
spirit.   Christ's filial relation to His then experience
in the wilderness, is regarded by the enemy as incon-
gruous, and so He is tempted to assert His rights and
to claim His privileges.   This Jesus declined to do,
just because He is fully possessed of the filial spirit.
So it is with ourselves.   The final test of the filial
spirit is unquestioning and glad acceptance of the will
of our Father, both in poverty and in plenty.

(ii) Passing from the primary significance, let us
notice, in the second place, the *immediate significance*
of the temptation.   This consists in the proposition
to gratify the pangs of hunger.   This temptation fell

in the field of physical nature and had nothing to do with right or wrong, though it might easily be made an occasion of wrong. Hunger is typical of all the elementary needs of life, and the petition, 'Give us this day our daily bread,' sums up in itself all our bodily needs. It is not a sin to hunger, and it is not a sin to appease hunger, but the doing so in the present circumstances would have been a very real sin. Innocent and necessary wants may be the devil's levers to overturn our souls. All our bodily appetites and natural cravings should be gratified only in the will of God and for His glory; never at the instigation of the devil or the selfish motions of the flesh. What was it that made this temptation so dangerous? This, first of all: that it was a temptation to doubt the providential care of God. The insinuation was that such a state of need did not become so exalted a Person, and betokened neglect on the part of God. The line of argument was, 'Fatherhood involves the primary responsibility to provide bread. Your Father is able to do this, but He has not done it. How, therefore, can you trust Him any longer? This evidence of God's neglect should lead you to give up your reliance upon Him.' That lies aback of the insinuation made to Adam and Eve in Eden—the insinuation that God was acting contrary to their highest interests. 'God doth know that in the day ye eat therof your eyes shall be opened, and ye shall be as gods, knowing good and evil.' It is a temptation to judge of our relation to our Father, and the Father's relation to us, by our outward and temporal circumstances, instead of by our inward and spiritual consciousness; and such a temptation as that, yielded to, is ever destructive of faith.

To Christ, it was, further, a temptation to deny His dependence upon God. Here the stress was upon the claim that He was the Son of God. If so, He had both the right and the power to act for His own comfort at such a time without reference to His Father. The devil proposes that He should cut short the discipline necessary for the accomplishment of the Divine will, and so struck at the very root of the mission on which Christ had come. It was a temptation for Jesus to separate Himself from us in our necessary dependence upon God, and by the use of a power which was His, but is not ours, and which was given Him not for His own self-preservation but for our salvation; to take from underneath us the ground on which alone we could claim kinship with Him. Had He, in the way suggested, supplied His needs, He would have snapped the bond of brotherhood between Himself and us by calling in resources which are not available to us. But He would not shake off for His own sake the human conditions which He had taken upon Him for our sakes. He had merged His lot with the lot of humanity, and He would not go back upon it. We might illustrate this by the story of Cato, who poured out the drop of water that had been brought to him from the African desert because it could not be shared with his men; or by the story of Alexander the Great, who shared all the privations and misfortunes, and took all the hazards of his great army, because he would be their true leader. So Christ resolutely declined to be drawn on to the ground of His Sonship for this conflict. He stood firm on the ground of His humanity, because He was fighting a battle that not only would minister to His own self-discipline but make Him for ever our representative and champion.

But again, Jesus was tempted here to demonstrate that He was the Son of God. This is closely akin to the former, and struck at the whole significance of the Incarnation. 'He took upon Him the form of a bond-slave, being made in the likeness of men, being found in fashion as a man,' and now He is tempted to act, not as a God-enabled man, but as the Son of God. The bottom motive of the devil seems to have been to prevent Him starting on His redeeming mission by getting Him to snap the connection between Himself and us.

The subtlety of this temptation is observable alike in its conception and deliverance, being exactly adapted to Jesus' condition, character and claims. As to His condition, He was suffering the pangs of hunger; as to His character there was nothing sinful, as I have said, in being hungry, or desiring bread; and as to His claims, had He not recently been declared to be the Son of God? All through it was a temptation to do a right thing. There was no direct or open appeal to sin, for that could have carried no hope of success. John had said that God could make children of Abraham out of these stones. Why should not Jesus make bread out of them? The real motive of the enemy was thickly veiled. It was a temptation to do a right thing in a wrong way. It was right for Jesus to satisfy His hunger, but not by the use of power given Him for other ends—a use which would have been an abuse.

We have not always the right to do all that we can. There are two great Christian laws, by one or other of

which we must be governed—the law of liberty, and
the law of love. Christ lived not by the former, but
by the latter. He would never make an unholy use
of power. To possess unlimited power for specific
ends and refrain from using it to our own advantage,
even in a pressing and apparently innocent cause, is
an ideal of virtue which it would be vain to expect in
any ordinary man. No temptation is more difficult
to resist than the prompting to do what seems needful
for self-preservation when abundant means are in
our hands.

But this was a temptation, further, to do a right
thing at the wrong time. Jesus sooner or later must
satisfy His hunger, even as He came to satisfy
the deeper hunger of the world, but the time had
not yet come. He was soon to work a miracle to
feed others. Why, then, would He not feed Himself?
But, no, His miracles shall all be for the needs of men,
not for His own. Satan tempted Jesus to begin where
it was His intention to end. It was a temptation to
premature realisation, and therein lay the evil of it.
In our Lord's refusal to do this is involved the con-
demnation of every plan for redressing the hard lot of
humanity which does not grow out of a moral root,
which seeks to make us happier without making us
holier. For the doing of every right thing there is a
right time, but that is never the devil's time.

Once more. It was a temptation to do a right
thing from a wrong motive—to turn stones into bread,
not only because He needed bread but to prove that
He could so do. Jesus never did anything to show
that He could do it. He did not perform His miracles
as a conjuror, but as a Redeemer. Our gifts and

capacities are not for glory, but for use; they are not for self-preservation, but for service. The use we make of power possessed reveals us. Our gifts and powers are given us for service and not for show. We must lose ourselves if we are ever to find ourselves. It is always the motive that gives the action its quality; and there is a great deal of good done in the Church which will never receive Divine recognition or reward, because it is robbed of its worth by unworthy motive. Like Jesus, we are all tempted to doubt the providential care of God, to deny our absolute dependence upon God, and to demonstrate that we can act without God. We are all tempted to seek right ends by wrong means, to secure at the beginning what can come to us only at the end, and to serve the Divine purposes from purely human motives.

(iii) But this experience of Christ's has not only a primary, and an immediate, but also *an ultimate significance*. This presents itself in the problem of how to make the most of life. Jesus was confronted with a choice of courses, and for us all, the moral problem reduced to its lowest terms, is that of making right choices. We are perpetually confronted with the necessity of selecting one out of two or more alternative courses. Life, as we have to face it, is a very complex thing, in which the threads of good and evil are bewilderingly intertwined, and to make a straight course in so wild a labyrinth is no easy task. Each of us is given a task to do, and we have but one life in which to carry it through. How are we going about it? That is the problem. The principle of the devil's proposition is to achieve apparent success at the cost of real success. This is a subtle and widespread peril, and the people

who fall to it are usually the envy of others. Here is
a man who makes a success of everything he attempts;
everything he touches seems to turn to gold. His
friends congratulate him and tell him he has conquered the world. Has he? Or has the world
conquered him? Have his successes helped him to
seek God; have they enriched his faith, hope and love;
have they made him a better citizen, a truer husband,
a wiser and kinder father, a humbler, sweeter Christian? Or have his successes but turned him into a
mere money-bag, or a safe-deposit vault? We shall
not forget the case of the rich fool. Such life-victories
are the worst defeats. They remind one of a story
about a soldier who shouted to his comrades, through
the darkness, that he had caught a prisoner. His
officer shouted back, 'Bring him in!' The answer
came, 'He won't come!' The officer said, 'Then come
yourself!' and the reply came, 'He won't let me!'
There are many men who count themselves victors
when they are but the prisoners of their very successes.
Beware of apparent success which is at the cost of real
success. Covet rather that apparent failure which is,
as a matter of fact, true success.

Further, this is a temptation to give the material
precedence over the spiritual. This is an ever-
present and insistent temptation, a temptation to
beggar the soul by feeding the body. It is never right
to starve our spiritual nature to get daily bread. Our
first duty is to God, not to ourselves. We had better
any day starve than commit a single sin to get bread.
Bread-making is not the primary object of a redeemed
soul. The cry, 'But a man must live,' is a delusion.
There is no necessity for us to live, but there is an

eternal necessity that we do right. The temptation to enthrone the material over the spiritual, and the human over the Divine, and the temporal over the eternal, is the greatest peril of our time. It is a temptation to satisfy the stomach by starving the soul. The prime temptation of millions resolves itself into a matter of bread, and to employ improper means to secure it. But we dare not obtain bread anyhow and at any price. Bread, let us remember, here stands for all the things that are material, the ways and means of life and the ends and objects that men so eagerly pursue.

But the devil's overture goes beyond even this, and would lead us to abandon faith in the interests of security. This is a temptation which presents itself not only to the Christian but to the Church. Faith, on the plane of nature, is our capacity for taking risks, and it is faith that we are losing in our modern passion for security. The element of adventure and romance is being abstracted from life because we no longer dare to take great risks. We prefer the ignoble prose of the solid earth, and we put our trust in our investments. It is an eclipse of faith which causes many people to stake a great deal more on feeding the poor than on preaching the Gospel to them, and which leads men to rate bread higher than the Bible. This strikes at the very root of things. The supreme need of our generation is of a vision of God as sovereign and sufficient to meet all the needs alike of body, soul and spirit, of the individual, of the Church, of the nation, and of the race. But the world to-day—and it is to be feared to a large extent the Church also—is trading on the rejected programmes of Jesus Christ.

Now let us think for a few moments of the secret of Christ's triumph, and first of all of the ground on which Christ stood. It was the ground of His humanity. 'Man shall not live by bread alone.' He fought this battle as man, and for man. Had He assumed the ground of His Sonship, as He was tempted by Satan to do, He would have evaded a necessary human experience and broken the bond which binds Him to ourselves. But He would have the enemy know, and us too, that though He faced the onslaught as man, He was not therefore left without succour. It was to the people in the wilderness, and for their encouragement, that the words were first spoken which Jesus here quotes. Satan had said, 'If Thou be the Son of God.' The answer comes back swiftly, 'Man shall not live by bread alone.' By saying 'man' Christ places Himself in relation to us and in dependence upon God; and it was both these positions that He was tempted to abandon.

Observe the weapon with which Christ fought. It was the Word of God. And mark His estimate of the Writings. They were to Him the words of God, wholly true and wholly to be trusted. The formula, thrice-repeated, 'It is written,' is assurance enough that He regarded the words quoted as of Divine origin and authority, and divinely designed to furnish guidance to everyone in circumstances such as confronted Him. Significantly enough, all His quotations are taken from a book which has long been a storm-centre of rationalistic criticism. As though anticipating this, our Lord sets His imprimatur upon it, and without controversy believes it to be the word of God. In determining the trustworthiness of any part of the

Bible we must regard not only its claims for itself, but also its power in action. Let us not fail to appreciate the fact that the first word spoken by Christ in His ministerial office is an assertion of the authority of Scripture; that He opposed the Word of God to the words of the devil. The readiness with which Christ quotes these Scriptures reflects the habit of His life from earliest days. During those long, silent years at Nazareth Jesus would daily and diligently study the Old Testament writings, storing away in His mind their precious truths, so that whenever the need arose He would be able to draw sharp arrows from His quiver against His enemies. In no other way and with no other weapon can we be prepared for the conflict. The devil does not announce his onslaughts upon us; he will not give us time to look for texts. Our only hope is in being fully equipped, and with sword in hand. Here we have a great argument for memorising Holy Scripture.

Mark, further, Christ's use of the Writings. In repelling the assaults of the devil our Lord did not appeal to inward illumination, but to written revelation. The word to which He refers is not that which was spoken to Him by His Father six weeks before, but that which was written fourteen hundred years before. He came to the devil as David went to Goliath, with weapons that were despised and looked upon with contempt. David took five smooth pebbles from the brook. Jesus took five books from the Bible. David slung one stone and down came the enemy. Jesus dealt with the devil with one book and brought him down, and had four to spare. This weapon is mighty equally for offence and defence. One dexterous thrust will inflict a mortal wound. Of course, any sort of use of Scripture will not do. There should always be, as in this instance, the existence of a true parallel between the case of those to whom the words were first addressed, and that of the person applying their teaching to his own case. Only so can the interpretation and application of Scripture be preserved from being fanciful, forced or false.

We have observed the ground on which Christ stood, and the weapon with which He fought, and won, and now a last word is in reference to the truth by which He won. 'Man shall not live by bread alone, but by every word that proceedeth out of the mouth of God.' The common interpretation given to these words is that which makes them to mean that man's soul is at all times of more consequence than his body; that whatever his physical wants may be, God can and always will sustain his spirit by His eternal Word. Such an interpretation entirely misses the point of the passage, and extracts from its force. The original context is this. 'The Lord suffered them to hunger, and fed them with manna, that He might make them to know that man doth not live by bread alone, but by every word that proceedeth out of the mouth of God.'. . God, by the ordinary operation of His providence, brings forth food for man out of the earth, but He is able to give sustenance in other ways if He sees fit so to do. Elijah was fed by the ravens. The meal did not fail in the barrel, nor the oil in the cruse. A hundred men were fed on twenty loaves of barley. Twenty thousand people, probably, were fed on five barley loaves and two small fishes. Israel was miraculously fed in the wilderness for forty years. Jesus was miraculously sustained for forty days. Extraordinary circumstances give us the right to look to God for extraordinary help. If He does not supply our need in one way, He will do it in another; if not by material means, then, as in the case of Jesus, and in response to trust, by the power of His will. This principle, as Godet says, is only the application of a living monotheism to the sphere of physical life. We should allow no physical necessity ever to compel us to deny our Father's providential care, or doubt our entire dependence upon Him.

The impact of Satan's suggestion struck against the trust life of Christ, as it will strike against ours, and it will be well if we learn what He here so plainly demonstrated—that the prompt and abundant supply of the lower and material demands of life does not constitute a trustworthy standard by which to determine either the fact or the measure of God's interest or care. Prosperity may be but an advertisement of failure, and adversity may be the highway to success. There is no promise that, in a worldly sense, the good will be prosperous; but there is abundant evidence that by testing is trust made triumphant. God will spread for us, as He did for Jesus, a table in the wilderness in response to the trust which was exhibited by the Master. Such trust must be maintained along the whole line of our physical need, and it will ever secure the vanquishment of the devil. But, as has been well said, he who would believe in Christ must believe in Him in spite of hunger, pain and suffering.

We have seen, then, that this first temptation is made on the lowest plane of our nature. Even the devil exhibits economy of his powers, and he will not make subtler efforts upon our higher nature if he can succeed on lower ground. His appeal to us on this level, the level of the senses, the level of the body, the level of things temporal and material, comes with terrific force and in manifold ways. It comes to us at all stages of life, and for his purpose in forms suitable, sometimes refined, sometimes gross. However and whenever he comes we should be found prepared, and the only true preparation is in the recognition that our bodies belong to God, and in the complete dedication of the same to Him. 'I beseech you therefore, by the mercies of God, that ye present your bodies a living sacrifice, holy, acceptable unto God, which is your reasonable service.' If that be done, Satan's temptation of us on that plane will fail, as it failed in the case of Christ. But he will not be routed and driven from us on that account. He returned to Jesus a second time, and then a third, and he will come back to us again and again. As he left Christ at last only for a season, we can never be sure that we have finally done with the devil. But let us, on every plane, and from every angle, and with reference to every form of temptation, however, whenever, wherever it may be presented—let us, as God-enabled, Spirit-filled men and women, stand where Jesus stood, and Satan shall shiver before the onslaughts of the eternal Word of God upon him.

3

TEMPTATION TO PRESUMPTION

THE account, in Matthew's Gospel, of the second temptation reads: 'Then the devil takes Him to the holy city, and sets Him upon the wing of the temple, and says to Him, If Thou art the Son of God, cast Thyself down: for it has been written, To His angels He will give charge concerning Thee, and on their hands shall they bear Thee, lest, haply, Thou strike Thy foot against a stone. Jesus said to him, Again it has been written, Thou shalt not tempt the Lord thy God.'

In the third Gospel the second temptation in Matthew's order, is put third: 'And he led Him to Jerusalem, and set Him upon the wing of the temple, and said to Him, If Thou art the Son of God, cast Thyself down hence: for it has been written that to His angels He will give charge concerning Thee, to guard Thee, and that on their hands they shall bear Thee, lest, haply, Thou strike Thy foot against a stone. Jesus answering said to him, It has been said, Thou shalt not tempt the Lord thy God.'

Let us keep steadily in mind that Jesus was being tested by temptation; that in this experience He was being operated upon both by the Holy Spirit and the Evil Spirit; the action of the one being regulative, and of the other subordinate; the one being the author, and the other the agent of this dispensation. The experience, therefore, may be regarded and interpreted from opposite standpoints—either as a test directed by God to make manifest Christ's worthiness, or as a temptation presented by the devil to compass Christ's fall. It may be well for us also to remember that while every test is not a temptation, every temptation is a test, and the two are frequently, as here, combined. In the first temptation the fact of Christ's faith in God was made evident; but in this, the second temptation, the quality of that faith is disclosed.

It is quite natural to ask, Is this experience of Christ's to be regarded as having been presented literally or ideally? Towards an answer to that question let us remember that the story of the temptation is told, not in the language of philosophy or psychology, but is addressed to the imagination, the reason and the conscience. We must be careful not to set *real* over against *actual* or *ideal*, for both these may be real. It is quite a mistake to suppose that nothing can be real that is not material. Whether the presentation of these temptations be conceived of as objective, or as subjective, they certainly were terrific in reality. It matters little, for the essential significance of the ordeal, whether this temptation was experienced in vision in the wilderness, or by transference to the temple in Jerusalem. Both views are reverently held. The one thing that is not open to dispute is, that the temptations were tragically real to Jesus.

Nor must we overlook the significance of the change of scene. The places in which our Lord was tempted are symbolic. The wilderness tells of a state and experience of depression more or less common to us all. We are all familiar with the wilderness as to experience. The mountain tells of a state and experience of ecstasy, of rapturous transport, the lot of the comparative few. But the city tells of the normal state and experience of man. In all these places and circumstances we shall be tested by temptation. Or we may speak of the wilderness as specially representing our discipline. It is there that we receive our severe training for future service, as did Moses by Horeb previous to his deliverance of Israel, as did Jesus here before entering upon His great ministry. The mountain, on the other hand, is symbolic of devotion. We rise to the heights for communion with God. But the city speaks to us rather of our duty. By means of discipline, devotion and duty alike, the enemy will make his onslaughts upon our souls. Our circumstances may change, but the tempter is ever at hand. How many have gone into the desert, thinking that they would escape temptation, but it has found them out. By escaping from men we do not escape demons, and it is needless to say that we shall meet with these at every turn and in every circumstance in the city.

Observe also how crafty are the methods of the devil. He is not limited to any one line of assault, but adapts himself to the situation. The temptation now swings to the opposite extreme. If Jesus will not live, if He will not turn stones into bread for the sustenance of His body and live, then let Him die. This is a possible interpretation of the event, as though Satan said, 'If I cannot get Him to be disloyal to God, I will endeavour to get Him out of the way altogether, or, at least, by the perversion of His trust in God, to render Him useless for the purpose of His mission.' We must see the first and second temptations in relation to one another. In these two assaults the enemy tempts Christ, first to distrust God, and then to a false trust in God; first to independence of Him—'Look after yourself; God has neglected you for forty days!'—and then, after having failed, to an unwarrantable dependence upon God—'Cast yourself down, and God will take care of you.' Our Lord was here tempted, first, to disregard the word of God, and then to put that word to severe proof. First of all, the devil designed to rob Christ of faith, and then he endeavoured to turn His faith into sin. So he adapts the temptation to the conditions and the circumstances. Satan learned from the result of the first assault how to make the second. Would that we were as quick to profit by our experience. Bishop Andrewes says, 'Out of Christ's conquests the devil makes a new assault. That is, since He will needs trust, he will set Him on trusting; he will trust as much as He will.' Bishop Hall speaks here to great purpose: 'If we be in extremes, it is all to one end—to mislead us to evil. If we cannot be driven down to despair, he labours to lift us up to presumption. It is not one foil that can put this bold spirit out of countenance. Temptations, like waves, break one in the neck of another. While we are in this warfare we must make count that the repulse of one temptation doth but invite another.' So we shall consider first of all, the subtle assault, and then the crushing reply.

THE SUBTLE ASSAULT.

1.—Jesus was here tempted, first of all, to indulge in idle presumption under the guise of trust in God. 'Cast Thyself down, for it is written.' This is a proposition which makes a powerful appeal to many. It is a temptation, for instance, to spiritual pride. Satan first appealed to Christ to exercise His power, and that having failed he now appeals to Him to exhibit His faith. In both, the temptation was to a misuse, first, of His power for self-preservation, and then of His power for self-glorification. Our very blessings are our perils. We may be proud of our spiritual life, proud of our spiritual success, and even proud of our humility. When the seventy came back to Christ they exclaimed, 'Lord, even the demons are subject unto us through Thy Name.' He replied, 'Rejoice not that the spirits are subject unto you, but rather rejoice because your names are written in heaven.' That is, Rejoice without pride. We should avoid rapture, if rapture puts us off our spiritual balance. Dutiful obedience is better than rapturous joy. We should be specially watchful in our high and holy places, and nowhere more so than when our pinnacle is on the temple. This is a temptation which, like a blight, attacks our best efforts in the bloom. It is a sort of parasite that fastens on our virtues as they ripen. We are most vulnerable where we are strongest. Moses, the meekest, spake unadvisedly. Elijah, the boldest of the prophets, fled for his life. Peter, the most loyal of disciples, denied his Lord.

2. But, further, this was a temptation to tempt Providence. There is a world of difference between faith and presumption. For Jesus to cast Himself from the temple pinnacle would have been not to trust, but to tempt God. There was ample occasion for Him, as there is for us, to exhibit trust. But to devise experiments, to leave the path of duty for the

sole purpose of putting God to the proof, would have been to exhibit the weakness of faith, and not its strength. It is not for us to seek circumstances of difficulty that grace and power might abound, but rather to avoid danger whenever we seek our Father's care, and His answer may come in successful avoidance rather than in rescue. If you are where God puts you, He will meet you where you are. God's promised protection is available not in paths of our own choosing, but only where He has sent us. Abraham and Joseph both went down into Egypt, the one contrary to the will of God, and the other according to the will of God. We shall have marked that Abraham was not preserved from the consequences of his own folly, but Joseph was divinely safeguarded in the midst of abounding perils. God sends some people to certain difficult and dangerous places, and undertakes to keep them there, to deliver them there from the power and conquest of the enemy. But, if we deliberately go to these places we cannot claim His promises. It were mere presumption to draw drafts on the faithfulness of God which we have no Scripture warrant to justify us in believing that He will honour. No one is safe in self-sought danger. God's promises are for us only when we are in the way and will of God. Quaint Mr. Trapp has observed that, in his day, the King was bound to protect travellers upon his highway between certain hours. 'But,' said he, 'he did not promise to protect them out of the King's highway, nor did he promise to protect them in it if they travelled at all hours, for instance, at dead of night.' So Abram's servant says, 'I being in the way, the Lord led me.' But He will never lead

us if we are out of the way. We must
be in His path and move in it at His time
and at His pace, if we would have His
protection, and claim His promises. 'It is a
precious doctrine,' says Spurgeon, 'that the saints are
safe, but it is a damnable inference from it that therefore they may live as they list. God gives us liberty,
not licence, and while He gives us protection He will
not allow us presumption. To trust God is faith, to
tempt God is presumption.' To throw ourselves
unnecessarily into perilous positions and expect God
to work a miracle for our protection is fanaticism and
not faith. When we rush into danger we should pray,
not for preservation but for pardon. God keeps us
in our ways only when they are His ways. It is useless
to trust God if we are off the path of duty. We have
no right to expect His protection in dangers which
we manufacture for ourselves. He who courts temptation invites his own ruin. He who trifles with danger
and then trusts to an unpledged protection, is guilty
of folly and presumption, God will not have us experiment upon Him, upon either His forbearance, protection, or power, He will keep His servants only in
lawful paths. His precepts are absolute, but His
promises are conditioned.

3. Yet once more. This was a temptation to
degrade ambition. Ambition in itself is not only not
wrong, but it is a high and noble quality. It can be
made wrong by having a false object, or by the employment of unworthy means for the realisation of a
right object. It was in this latter sense that the devil
would tempt Jesus to degrade His ambition. He was
the promised Messiah, and would, sooner or later,

be manifested and acknowledged. But He would not seek that acknowledgment or make that manifestation at the instigation of the devil. In other words, He would not take a short cut to fame. The noblest qualities may be misdirected and abused, and no one of them more easily than ambition. The highest ends are not reached by the shortest routes, and given a true object, the modern passion for speedy realisation is but a degradation of high aspiration.

But further, Jesus was here tempted to resort to vulgar sensation for the more rapid fulfilment of His mission. Those who regard this experience as having been objectively real see in it an attempt to get Christ to fulfil the expectation of His people, that the Messiah would head Israel from the pinnacle of the temple. If this be the case, then it was a temptation to satisfy vulgar expectation, and by sensational methods to establish Himself in the affections of the people. The Jews expected Christ to come in some startling way, in some dramatic fashion, as in a flash of glory from the temple. And the devil here would have Jesus lower His aims to common expectation and yield to the conceptions of the crowd. That is the essential significance, in part, of this temptation. It was a temptation to adopt the most showy and speedy way of fulfilling His ambitions; in other words, as I have said, to take a short cut to success. 'Make a show— the people love a show—and you will gain the end of your ambition at once; everybody will shout that you are Messiah.' But, let us remember that religious acrobatics are not calculated to serve the kingdom of God. It was never an end with Christ simply to appeal to men's sense of wonder. All His miracles were moral. But to have thrown Himself down from the pinnacle of the temple in response to vulgar expectation would have been immoral. God's will and work must be done in God's way. The crowd is always ready for a sensation, and, alas! there are always those who are disposed to stimulate religion by booming it, and to fill the churches by methods of sensationalism, to resort to spectacular display in order to popularise the Gospel. But it is still certain that if we depart from sanity to gain popularity, we win only notoriety. Our gifts and powers and opportunities are given us, not for show but for service. We are not called to be spiritual performers, but to walk humbly with God, to bear Him witness in a manner worthy of Him. But there are false and unworthy ways of bearing witness and furnishing evidence. Some methods, popular in our time, are unworthy of the Gospel. This is a temptation which comes especially to young ministers. Are you going to be the kind of preacher that the people wish? or are you willing to be God's messenger? The devil comes and tempts us in this way. Without a too scrupulous regard for the method, will you make a place and a name for yourself at the beginning of your career? Right at the start get the crowd, without being too particular as to how you get them? Or are you prepared by long toil, and perhaps by pain, possibly through contempt and rejection, possibly by emptying instead of by filling your church, to work your way to your vindication? This temptation comes to us all.

But yet again. Jesus was here tempted to abandon common-sense in the interests of a larger faith. Why sense is called common sense, seeing it is so rare, I have

never been able to find out! The first assault was
made upon the simplicity of Christ's trust in God;
but the second assault is made upon the sanity of that
trust. If Satan cannot break up the trust of Jesus he
will endeavour to lead it to unwarrantable lengths.
'Then,' you say, 'are we to take no risks? How are
we to distinguish between faith and presumption?'
Risks may and should be taken in the path of duty.
To do what is irrational is never of faith, unless there
is special Divine warrant for so doing. The soul, or
church, that takes no risks will never be progressive or
triumphant. We may and we should dare, but our
daring should always be in the path of duty. If God
sends us trouble He will give us enablement in it or
deliverance from it. But if we thrust ourselves into the
fire, or drink poison, Almighty God will not keep us
from the consequences. If Providence puts you or me
on the temple pinnacle, He will safeguard us there.
But if we deliberately throw ourselves down, instead of
going down by the steps provided, we shall be smashed
at the bottom. Faith must first and last be rational;
otherwise it becomes credulity, presumption, or super-
stition. Our risks must be rational risks. We are
never called upon to suppress reason in order to culti-
vate faith. To put our common-sense in abeyance in
the interests of spirituality is crass folly. Reason
without faith, of course, is essentially barren and fruit-
less. But faith without reason becomes a hot-bed for
all sorts of morbid, fungoid growths. God gives us
reason that faith may be kept sweet and strong, and He
will not preserve us from the consequences of fool-
hardiness and credulity, against which He has given
us means to defend ourselves. The angels will ever

watch over us with a tender care, when to accomplish a duty or to perform an act of self-denying love we confront peril. Not so when we presumptuously and for our own ends rush into danger.

This temptation to abandon common-sense is often felt in reference to physical daring and commercial venture. But is chiefly experienced in the field of morals. The ball-room, the theatre, the race-course, the card-table are not places for the cultivation of faith, and if the Christian puts himself in the way of these, he has no right to expect that God will despatch angels for his protection. We must never treat our faith as an experiment, instead of what it is—an experience. It is utter recklessness to rush into danger, physical or moral, and then trust that we shall come out unscathed. Such presumptuous trust is really presumptuous distrust.

But in still more subtle ways is this temptation presented. Take, for instance, the employment of material means for the healing of diseases of mind and body. God has put these within our reach, and He expects us to use such means, and there is evidence enough of the excellence of this practice. This is not to say that our trust is in the means, but in God, from Whom is the therapeutic principle resident in the means. To neglect such means is not to trust God, but to tempt Him. If we are beyond the reach of means, or if means have utterly failed, then we have a right, ever in perfect subjection to the will of God, to look to Him to perform a miracle; but not while legitimate means are within our reach which we decline to employ. God observes a strict economy of His powers.

This principle may also be applied to our spiritual

service, service in which the Holy Spirit has not under-
taken to do for us what He has made it possible for us
to do for ourselves. If we are going to speak God's
message to the people, we must prepare. We have got
to sweat our brains, and if we do not, we may call upon
the Holy Spirit to enable us, until we are black in the
face, and we shall be left high and dry at the last.
Said a young minister at the foot of the pulpit steps to
one of his members, 'You know, I never know, when
I get into the pulpit, what I'm going to say.' 'Yes,'
was the rejoinder, 'and when you come down nobody
knows what you have said!' We have a right to
expect God's help only in the way of discipline and
obedience. There is a point where trust may easily
pass into trespass, and where faith becomes folly. The
refusal to adopt reasonable means in order to desirable
and necessary ends is not trust, but presumption. On
the other hand, the employment of unreasonable
means in order to desirable and necessary ends, is not
trust, but audacity. It was to this that Jesus was
tempted, and this which He withstood, and it is this to
which we also are tempted, and, it is to be feared, to
which, too often, we succumb.

Now let us look for a moment or two at THE
CRUSHING REPLY. Here mark the ground of
Satan's assault. 'Cast Thyself down, for it is written.'
Jesus had just used the Scripture against him with
telling effect, and now Satan himself will use the text
—he will turn theologian and oppose Jesus with His
own weapons. 'What is this I see?' says Bishop Hall.
'Satan himself with a Bible under his arm and a text
in his mouth. "It is written, He shall give His angels

charge over Thee.'" Since the devil dared to touch
the sacred body of Christ with his hand, he may well
touch the Scriptures with his tongue. Yet, if his head
is full of Scripture, his heart is full of rebellion, as ours
also may be. Observe with what diabolical ingenuity
he uses the passage from the ninety-first Psalm for his
present purpose. He both misquotes and misapplies
it. The original passage reads, 'He shall give His
angels charge over Thee to keep Thee in all Thy
ways.' The last sentence the devil cunningly omits
and so changes the whole complexion of the passage.
From the temple pinnacle to the ground below was
not one of God's ways for Christ, and anyone taking it
did not come within the scope of the promise of His
protection. Satan made out that the promise was
unconditioned, and in this way he perverted the
Scripture. He would have Christ promise to Himself
more than God had pledged, and in this way, though
quoting a correct principle, he made of it a wrong
application. In his use of this weapon the devil has,
alas! been more successful with the professed followers
of Christ than he was with Christ Himself. There is
nothing more common than misquotation and mis-
application of Holy Scripture. Every heresy under
the sun can appeal to Scripture, after that fashion, in
proof of itself. Shakespeare makes Richard of Glou
cester twist the sacred text:

> But then I sigh; and with a piece of Scripture,
> Tell them that God bids us do good for evil:
> And thus I clothe my naked villainy.
> With odd old ends stol'n forth of holy writ;
> And seem a saint when most I play the devil,

A marred and mutilated Bible in our hands has no chance of ultimate success, no more chance now than it had in the wilderness. Neither by insertion nor excision can we ever hope either rightly to interpret or apply Scripture. The popular heresy that the Bible is not, but only contains, the word of God, is not of very aristocratic origin!

Mark the manner of Christ's reaction to this assault. 'It is written again.' He clinches Scripture ill-used by Scripture well-used. We may not so expound one verse of Scripture that it is repugnant to another. The plan of building theological or moral opinions on isolated fragments and texts of Scripture may be used to support any heresy or any crime. We must regard as an infallible canon of interpretation, that all that Scripture has to say on any given subject is the truth about that subject. And so, if Scripture be compared with Scripture it will be found consistent in all its parts. Jesus met a promise misused with a precept properly applied, and at that moment the precept was worth more to Christ than the promise. 'Sometimes a precept is a necessary counteracting principle to guard us from the perversion of a promise. Promises are like sweetmeats given to children, which, too profusely eaten, bring on sickness. But the precept comes in as a healthy tonic, so that you may feed upon the promise without injury.' And so Satan's, 'It is written,' is responded to by Jesus' 'It is written again, Thou shalt not tempt the Lord thy God.' The passage in Deut. vi., from which these words are taken is: 'Ye shall not tempt the Lord your God, as ye tempted him in Massah.' Going back to Ex. xvii. for this occasion, we learn that the sin of Israel at Rephidim

was that of questioning the presence of God with them, until they saw a supernatural proof of it. Jesus was here tempted to put God to such a proof. To have done so would have been an evidence both of folly and unbelief on His part. Satan tried to divert Christ from the true path of trust, and 'craftily camouflaged that path at the point of divergence with Scripture paint,' but all to no purpose. Swiftly and severely Jesus replied: 'To fall from this sacred edifice to the valley below would not be to trust God, but to tempt Him, and this is forbidden.'

In quoting this Scripture, the Lord of the Scriptures changes it from the plural into the singular. 'Ye shall not tempt' becomes 'Thou shalt not tempt.' Almost certainly He means to say, 'Not only may I not tempt the Lord My God, but you may not tempt Me, the Lord your God. Desist, therefore, from tempting Me.' Once again the enemy is unsuccessful. He has failed to shake the simplicity of Christ's trust, and he has failed to corrupt its sanity. Christ repelled this onslaught by a declaration of His and our abiding dependence upon God for the maintenance of His and our physical life, and by a repudiation of any means for the accomplishment of His mission, which would be a provocation of His Father. As a Spirit-filled Man, Jesus went into this conflict, and as a Spirit-enabled Man He came out of it triumphant, not only for Himself but for us. Jesus did nothing with the tempter and with the temptation in the wilderness, that we here and now in every circumstance may not do both with him and with it. 'This is the victory that overcometh' alike the world, the flesh and the devil.

4

TEMPTATION TO COMPROMISE

THERE are two accounts, also, of the third temptation. Matt. iv. 8-10: 'Again, the devil takes Him to a mountain exceedingly high, and shows Him all the kingdoms of the world and their glory, and says to Him, All these things will I give to Thee, if, falling down, Thou wilt worship me. Then Jesus says to him, Get thee away, Satan: for it has been written, The Lord thy God shalt thou worship, and Him only shalt thou serve.'

Luke iv. 5-8: 'And he (the devil), leading Jesus up into a high mountain, showed Him all the kingdoms of the habitable world in a moment of time. And the devil said to Him, To Thee will I give all this authority and their glory: for to me it has been delivered, and to whomsoever I wish I give it. If therefore Thou wilt worship before me, all things shall be Thine. And Jesus answering him said, Get thee behind Me, Satan: for it has been written, Thou shalt worship the Lord thy God, and Him only shalt thou serve.'

We must observe in a preliminary word the order of the temptations; this differs in Matthew and in Luke. In Matthew the temple temptation precedes the mountain temptation. In Luke the order is reversed. Almost certainly Matthew's is the chronological order, being best suited to all the known facts. Three reasons for this conclusion may be given. First of all, Satan is not likely to have addressed Jesus as the Son of God, and then to have left that ground only to return to it later. The first two assaults upon Christ were made on the ground of His Divine Sonship 'If Thou be the Son of God,' and suffering defeat on that ground the devil at last abandoned it. Another reason for this conclusion is that it is incredible that any attack should have been made upon our Lord after His command, 'Get thee hence, Satan.' That is an authoritative and final word. And yet again, in Matthew's order there is observable a development in the subtlety and range of the temptations. The appeal in the first instance is to appetite. 'Make these stones bread.' In the second instance it is to adventure. 'Throw yourself down and trust God.' In the third instance it is to ambition. 'Worship me, and I will give you all the kingdoms of the world and their glory.' The first was a temptation to doubt, the second was a temptation to presume, and the third was a temptation to treason against God. The first temptation was made on the plane of the body, the second was made on the plane of the soul, and the third was made on the plane of the spirit. So there is a heightening of the level of the temptation, and with the heightenng a growing subtlety. The bait in the first temptation was Christ's personal need. The bait in the second was the Jewish nation. 'If you fall down and trust God the people will welcome you and acclaim you the long-looked-for Messiah.' But the bait in the third instance was the whole world. 'All these things will I give Thee and the glory of them.'

Let us look first of all, at Satan's final assault, and then at Christ's crowning victory.

Observe here, first of all, the nature and the ground of this temptation. There is presented to our Lord a vision of kingship. As to the presentation, itself, we inevitably ask, how are we to conceive of the vision? Was it actual and literal? Or was it ideal and spiritual? Was the vision presented outwardly or inwardly? Was it objective? Or was it subjective? That question arises with reference to the Temptation considered as a whole, as well as to its various parts. Four answers may be given to this enquiry. There are those who hold that the vision was actual, literal, outward, objective. There are those, again, who hold that it was ideal, inward, subjective, spiritual. There are those who think that these two must be blended, that it was both literal and ideal; that is, that from a Canaan or Syrian height Jesus was given to see the surrounding lands and their glory, and that in imagination He saw in these all that they represented. There are others, again, who feel that the manner of the temptation cannot be known, and this view is reflected in Milton's words:

> By what strange parallax or optic skill
> Of vision, multiplied through, air or glass
> Of telescope, were fruitless to enquire.

The one thing, as I have said before, that must be insisted on everywhere, and always maintained, is, that the temptation was to Jesus tragically real.

We must take time to be impressed by the grandeur of this vision. From not a few heights in Palestine a glorious view can be obtained. Edersheim says: 'Jesus and the devil stand on the top of some very high mountain. It is in the full blaze of sunlight that He

now gazes upon a wondrous scene. Before Him rise
from out the cloud-land, at the edge of the horizon,
forms, figures, scenes—come words, sounds, har-
monies. The world in all its glory, beauty, strength,
majesty, is unveiled. Its work, its might, its greatness,
its art, its thought emerge into clear view, and still
the horizon seems to widen as He gazes, and more
and more, and beyond it still more and still brighter
appears.'

Nor must we fail to appreciate the allurement of
this vision. How great an appeal this temptation
made to Christ we can only imagine by thinking of
the appeal which the prospect of doing universal good
would make to the noblest minds. Being a temptation of widest range, its force must have been corre-
spondingly greater than that of the other temptations.
What was offered to Christ was authority and glory,
and the offer was made to One Who had a right to
the one, and was worthy of the other. No temptation
is so great as that which appeals to our consciousness
of capacity, and the belief that for certain ends we are
ordained. Jesus saw everywhere the traces of a lost
magnificence, a nobler destiny, an underlying capacity
for greater things, yea, everywhere a half-conscious
yearning for deliverance, appealing to His great
heart of love. With powers fitted to grapple with
such giant miseries, should He be content to pass His
life as a simple private man? Or should He not at
once take to Himself His rightful power? There is
the line of allurement of this temptation. Such was
the vision that presented itself to our Lord.

With it there came the promise of kingship. Mark
the scope of this promise. 'I will give Thee all this

authority and the glory of the kingdoms.' This the enemy said, having showed Him all the kingdoms of the inhabited world. It was a promise of worldwide empire, of majesty and power beyond all that Alexander had once attained, beyond all that Tiberius then possessed. How tempting was the prospect! It was implied that Jesus could use these kingdoms for the best interests of the human race; that He could and would put down cruelty, and avarice, and lust, and oppression which reigned rampant in the world; that He would improve the condition of the poor; that He would put a stop to war and to violence and to bloodshed, and introduce universal peace and happiness. Jesus knew that He was a King and that the glory was His by right, and that the world would be blessed under His rule; and now the opportunity seemed within His grasp to take to Himself His rightful power and reign.

Was this promise all an empty boast? Was it but a devil's impertinence? No, for he said, 'It hath been delivered unto me,' and father of lies though he be, his falsehoods are well mixed with truth. Jesus did not dispute this claim, and had there been no truth in it there had been no force in it. This opens a wide and profoundly interesting subject, namely, the devil's relation to and power over this world. His utterance is at once a claim and an acknowledgment—a claim that the world's kingdoms are his, and an acknowledgment that they are his by grant, that they have been delivered unto him, and are not his by essential right, and therefore are not his in perpetuity.

The acknowledgment raises the questions, Who delivered the kingdoms to him, when were they delivered to him, why were they delivered to him, and for how long have they been delivered to him? The claim raises the questions, To what extent is it true that the kingdoms are his, in what ways is his power over them manifested; how can this claim be reconciled with the sovereignty of God; what is the relation and what should be the attitude of the Christian and of the Church to this fact? I do not propose to enter into these questions. Enough for our present purpose to mark that the offer of the kingdoms to Jesus was not a meaningless overture, but a real temptation. Satan is 'the god of this world,' 'the prince of the power of the air,' and in defeating humanity in Eden he obtained a kingly possession and power over this world, of which Christ, the second Man, the last Adam, came to deprive him. The offer presented itself to Jesus as a chance so to do, and therein lay its power and its subtlety. How great was the force of this promise, 'I will give it Thee.' Satan not only claims possession, but the power to delegate, to sub-let the kingdoms of the world. While there is a sense in which this claim is false, there is a sense, undoubtedly, within limits, in which it is true. Not absolutely, but relatively, he can give the kingdoms, not by sacrificing his power, but by vesting it in agents. He now had no intention of sacrificing his power. He intended certainly to make Jesus his agent and to vest his power in Him, and so to degrade the very Son of God.

Such a temptation could be presented only to one conscious of great power and high destiny. Smaller baits would do for smaller souls. Here Bishop Andrewes is at his best. It is not often that he expresses himself in irony so fine and so effective as he does in one of his sermons on the Temptation. Contrasting this offer of the kingdoms to Christ, and rejected by Him, with paltry bribes, the mess of pottage, the Babylonish garment, the two changes of raiment, the thirty pieces of silver, for which we are so often contented to barter all, he says, 'There be some that will say they were never tempted with kingdoms. It may well be, for it needs not when less will serve. It was Christ only Who was thus tempted. In Him lay a heroical mind that could not be allured with smaller matters. But with us it is nothing so, for we esteem far more basely of ourselves. We set our wares at a very easy price; he may buy us even "dagger-cheap," as we say. He need never carry us so high as the mount. The pinnacle is high enough, yea, the lowest steeple in all the town would serve the turn. Or let him but carry us to the leads and gutters of our own houses; nay, let us but stand in our windows or our doors, if he will give us, but so much as we can there see he will tempt us thoroughly; we shall accept it and thank him too. He shall not need to come to us with kingdoms. If he would come to us with thirty pieces, I am afraid many of us would play Judas. Nay, less than so much would buy a great sort, even handfuls of barley and pieces of bread. Yea, some will not stick to buy and sell the poor for a pair of shoes, as Amos speaketh. A matter of half-a-crown, or ten groats, a pair of shoes, or some such trifle will bring us on our knees to the devil.'

The largeness of the bribe is evidence that the devil knew Whom he was tempting, and that if he had won here he would have secured a victory immeasurably

greater than the one he gained in Eden. As the bribe
was the largest the devil had to offer, so the temptation
was the most powerful in its appeal to such a one as
Christ. The devil, however, never fulfils his promises.
He is a liar and the father of lies. He offered Jesus
all the kingdoms only to rob Him of them. He
promised the world to Alexander and he gave him a
profligate's grave. He said to Napoleon the Great,
'Bow down and worship me, and all shall be thine.'
Napoleon did it, and the devil gave him St. Helena.
He offered the Kaiser a place in the sun, and he gave
him a coward's captivity. With less prizes he tempts
you and me, but he is bent not on our enrichment
but on our ruin. The sparkling cup is hell-poisoned,
the ravishing pleasure will bring exquisite pain.

Having presented the vision of the kingdoms, and
having made the promise of them, he lays down the
condition of kingship. 'If Thou wilt fall down and
worship me.' Why would the devil sell all the world
kingdoms for such a price as that? It is not the
biggest coins that have the largest value. In the
transaction Jesus stood to lose all, and the devil stood
to gain all. Jesus was here tempted to sell principle
for property and power, and these are never of com-
mensurate value. Yet men, not altogether mean, or
base, or without noble aspirations, have before now
made this bargain for the good that they could do,
persuading themselves that the righteous end justified
the unrighteous means. But, beginning in good
faith, they have found that the bargain has carried
them further than they ever intended to go, and have
found out their mistake when it was too late. There
are only two ways of obtaining ascendancy and leader-

ship among men—by force, or by persuasion; by the
sword, or by moral and intellectual influence.   Mo-
hammedanism and the Papacy have tried to unite
these, and with what results we know. Jesus said,
'If My Kingdom were of this world, then would My
soldiers fight.'   But it was not. He came to establish
a kingdom not by slaughtering, but by being slaugh-
tered; not by the sword, but by the sacrifice of Himself.
The condition was simple, but impossible; impossible
because of the nature of Christ's Kingdom, and
impossible because of the significance of the act
required.   Power and glory can be too dearly bought.
The kingdoms of the world are founded upon force
and maintained by fraud. Christ's Kingdom is far
otherwise. He needs no cruel arms to protect it,
or corrupt money to maintain it; for it is a kingdom
founded on righteousness and functioning in peace.
Satan's kingdom is without—Christ's is within; Satan's
kingdom is material—Christ's is spiritual; Satan's
kingdom is transient—Christ's is eternal.   Satan's
object here was to get Jesus to reverse the true means
for the establishing of His Kingdom, and so to fling it
away.   Milton represents Christ as saying:

> Victorious deeds
> Flamed in My heart, heroic acts—one while
> To rescue Israel from the Roman yoke,
> Men to subdue and quell o'er all the earth,
> Brute violence and proud tyrannic power,
> Till truth were freed and equity restored:
> Yet, held it more humane, more heavenly, first
> By winning words to conquer willing hearts,
> And make persuasion do the work of fear.

But Christ would not rely upon the devil's weapons,
on the weapons either of physical or material strength,

but only on the power of love and the force of truth.

I would have you notice, further, the subtlety and force of this temptation. There is here, from the devil, a recognition of the universal need. He admitted the world's need of a king, and of one who would be a benefactor. How many bleeding hearts were waiting to be bound by Him, how many who now sat in darkness were waiting for light from Him, what truths were waiting for Him to utter, what wrongs for Him to redress, what strongholds of oppression for Him to cast down. The power of accomplishing all this, of staunching all these fountains of tears, of imparting all this knowledge of His Father's love, of redressing the woes and wrongs of humanity, of destroying all the destroyers of the earth—this was the glory which the royalties of the world wore in His sight, and here was the force which this temptation presented. There could be no idea in Satan's mind but that Jesus would bless mankind, and this was an appeal to His power and His will so to do.

There is here an acknowledgment of Jesus' Messianic mission. The devil had been unable to touch Him as the Son of God. He had a knowledge of Who he had challenged, and of what was at stake. And with this recognition and acknowledgment came the suggestion that the world needed a joint kingship, that is, that both God and the devil had rights in humanity, that this human world could not be either wholly spiritual or wholly sinful, that it could not be either wholly good or wholly bad, that it could be neither wholly pure nor wholly vile; that what was needed was a recognition alike of Christ's and Satan's place and power over the human race, and that the ideal government would be one under a joint authority. By worshipping him Jesus would acknowledge his authority, and in return would receive from him the power and the glory of the kingdoms. But how impossible was such a compact. Christ's Kingdom was not to be the continuance of anything previously existing, but one entirely new. It was not to be material but moral. His and Satan's principles could never be reconciled; they were mutually exclusive. This subtle and ruinous idea is still presented for our acceptance, namely, that the kingdom within us should not be under one authority only, but that God should be acknowledged, and mammon also; that we should divide our devotion between the flesh and the spirit, between the world and the Church, between this life and the next; in other words, that we should endeavour to make the best and the most of both worlds. It is the temptation to a catholicity which is really a fatal compromise, whether it be made in the realm of thought or of action. It is a temptation to lower our standard in order to increase our reach, a temptation to endanger our integrity in order to enlarge our influence. It is ever present and insistent. The devil offered to Jesus the world. It was these kingdoms He had come to win, and the enemy, knowing this, threw himself in the line of Jesus' hope and purpose and proposed a short path to possession.

Let us now think of the peril and power of this temptation. It was a temptation to easy conquest. Jesus was bidden establish the kingdom at once without discipline and without sacrifice. This temptation comes to us all —to take the line of least resistance, to reach the crown by dodging the cross, to attain to power without sacrifice, to gratify ambition at the cheapest rate, to attain to sovereignty without suffering. The suggestion is that there is an easier way to conquest then by Calvary. That is a devil's lie. It is a temptation to take our ease and save our strength when the call of human need is stirring in our hearts and consciences. It was Peter's advice to Jesus, 'Spare Thyself, Lord,' and it drew from the Lord the same words which He uttered in reply to the devil here—because Peter spoke this at the instigation of the devil—and Jesus said, 'Get thee behind Me, Satan.'

Is there anything worth while ever attained or accomplished without cost? It was when Zion travailed that she brought forth children. There is no salvation without sacrifice, there is no short cut to real conquest. This is a temptation greatly to be resisted in our day. It is a temptation to sinful compromise. No one will be deceived by the temptation to adopt evil means for evil ends. But many have fallen to evil means for worthy ends. Jesus was here tempted to a treacherous act for a righteous cause— just to bow the knee to Satan in order to bless the world. It was an offer of a great good for a little evil. Yet to have yielded would have been high treason against God. It is a moral certainty that means correspond to ends and determine them. Yet men are constantly deceiving themselves with reference to this, by seeking moral and spiritual ends by physical and secular means, without perceiving the inconsistency. It is a question we all have to decide— whether we will seek by some compromise of truth, in our words and actions, for success and honour and applause among men; or whether, by obedience to the God of truth, we will pay the necessary price for the heavenly possession. The temptation to compromise comes to us all. It comes to the minister in his study, as he is preparing the sermon, it comes to the statesman in his cabinet, it comes to the doctor in his consulting-room, it comes to the author and editor at his table, it comes to the lawyer at his office, it comes to the employer in his business, it comes to the labourer at his work. Allow a little evil for the sake of a great good. It is the temptation to leave the straight line of duty, and service, and faithfulness, and truth, and loyalty, and conviction, and moral and spiritual integrity, to take the lower path of popularity, of honour, and of temporal success. To do this is to take a course which we may dignify by some fair name, but which in Scripture language is worshipping the devil. The spirit of compromise is everywhere in the world. It prompts us to be silent when we ought to speak, for fear of offending; it prompts us to praise when it is not deserved, to keep people our friends; it prompts us to tolerate sin and not to remonstrate, because so to do might give us enemies. What of the church which accepts the money of the brewer and then is lukewarm about temperance reform? What of the church that appoints men as its officers because of their money and their social position, rather than because of their spiritual qualifications; that lowers its standard of Christian morality for fear of alienating wealthy and powerful men? Is not such a church worshipping the devil? These, and many such like things, are done, and men comfort themselves by the cant phrases, 'It's no use trying to alter it; they all do it; it's the custom of the trade; one must live; do not be a faddist; the idea is Utopian; it cannot be helped.' This is virtually to say that evil is too strongly entrenched to be uprooted, and must be tolerated; and that if you are to get on in the world you must not be over-precise, or you will lose your influence and then do no good at all. Perish the thought!

The spirit of compromise is the handmaid of reaction and the herald of decline. Immoral compromise must be crushed to atoms in the right hand of obedience. It can never be right to do evil that good may come. The suggestion to get a position anyhow and then to use it for noble ends, is a Satanic temptation. Christ never won or used power otherwise than as God's will allowed. Nor should we. The devil asked Jesus to bow to him only once, and only once would have been necessary to compass His ruin. So we are tempted to give up our scruples and to bow with the rest—just a simple act, and only once. The devil whispers into your ear, and into mine, that we can have any sort of reserve we like in our own hearts, but bids us yield here and there in order to 'get on.'

If you cannot succeed without bowing to the devil, then make up your mind to fail, to be an unsuccessful man all your life, in the interests of loyalty; be willing to see others, weighted with fewer scruples, get before you in the race, and grasp the prizes. But you cling to your God; have none of the devil's short cuts to advantage or prosperity. Such, in the last analysis, is a temptation to abandon conscience. The temptation to silence the voice of conscience, to abandon strict integrity, is ubiquitous and persistent. When a man lowers the white banner of his purity and integrity, he has admitted the enemy into his citadel and broken with God. To win in these days means an uphill fight, but it must be faced.

> Though lone, the way as that already trod,
> Cling to thine own integrity and God;

turning your back on selfishness, the first temptation; on presumption, the second; and on compromise, the third.

Jesus now orders the enemy off the field, naming him. 'Get thou hence, Satan.' The devil now retreated from the scene, exhausted and defeated. He had assaulted Christ with every form of temptation, but his design had been apprehended and his subtleties laid bare. Christ did appease His hunger, but not by wilderness stones. Christ has manifested Himself to the world, but not by vulgar sensationalism. And He will yet rule over all the kingdoms of the earth, but not by the avoidance of discipline or of death. Whatever Textual Criticism may have to say about the doxology in what we call 'The Lord's Prayer,' until it is absolutely certain, beyond question, that it is not authentic, we are going to see the Temptation of our Lord reflected in the words, 'Thine is the kingdom'—which the devil offered Him and He despised; 'Thine is the power'—which the devil tempted Him to put forth and He declined; 'Thine is the glory'—which he bade Him seek from the crowd below by an act of trust, which really would have been distrust of His God.

All the things that He rejected at the hand of the devil He has obtained by suffering, by discipline, by death, by resurrection, by ascension, by the Holy

Spirit, by the Bible, by the Church, by you and by me. The Father's test succeeded, but the devil's temptation failed. Jesus' trust in God is revealed to be simple, sane, and strong. With calm and fixed decisiveness, He chose from the beginning, and trod until the end, with bleeding but unreluctant feet, the path of suffering, on His way to the throne. He Who did not fall to the scourge of poverty at the beginning, did not fall to the vision of plenty at the end. Adversity and prosperity, humiliation and exaltation alike found Him resolute and loyal. He Who had been anointed by the Spirit conquered by the Spirit; and the things which He rejected at the hands of the devil, He received from the hand of God.

There is no other way of victory for us, than that which was His. Whatever Jesus overcame, we can overcome. His was not only a triumph of humanity, but for humanity. There is no crown where there is no conflict; there is no triumph where there is no temptation. The way of victory for Christ was, in each instance, by absolute loyalty to God as revealed in His Word; and there is no other way for us.

Warfare, to be effective, must be scientific; so that the more we know of God, of ourselves, and of the world around us, the better shall we be prepared to resist all evil and to receive all good. Christ experienced and exhausted temptation of every kind, and on every plane. He did not merely not succumb, but He gloriously conquered, and so has made possible to you and to me continuous victory. The devil is routed, the devil is vanquished, and Christ's victory is yours and is mine. Let us then face him afresh, for he certainly will assault us as we go to our wilderness, or to the city, or to the mountaintop, in hours of discipline, and of devotion, and of duty—using the weapon with which Christ won, standing where Christ stood as a Spirit-filled and God-enabled man, conscious before we start that the victory has been won and that Christ has triumphed, so that we may boldly say, 'Thanks be unto God, Who giveth us the victory through our Lord Jesus Christ.'